Day Trading:

Beginner's Guide to Make Money with Day Trading

Warren Richmond

is not engaging in the rendering of legal, financial, medical or professional advice. The content of this book has been derived from various sources. Please consult a licensed professional before attempting any techniques outlined in this book.

By reading this document, the reader agrees that under no circumstances are is the author responsible for any losses, direct or indirect, which are incurred as a result of the use of information contained within this document, including, but not limited to, —errors, omissions, or inaccuracies.

Table of Contents

What This Book Will Teach You

Are you curious to learn about becoming a Day Trader but unsure where to start?

Have you always wanted to make money from Trading, but are intimidated by the technical jargon being used?

If these questions relate well with you, then this book is for you. In this book you will find the basic essentials to learning Trading. This book introduces readers to the "Day Trading," the in's and out, the various processes and steps involved in it.

Who this Book is for

This book contains information on how to learn Day Trading from a beginner level.

Readers who can benefit the most from the book include:

- Individuals interested in earning money from Day Trading

- Investing enthusiasts who want to learn Day Trading as another possible source of income

- Investors who would like to know more about the Trading side, beginning with Day Trading

How this Book is Organized

This book is organized into three parts. The parts are best read in chronological order. Once you become familiar with all the steps outlined in the book, you can go directly to the techniques which apply to your current situation the best.

The three parts of the book are:

Part One outlines the essential topics on Trading and Investing, and then Day Trading in particular. The section also talks about how important it is to learn these topics as a beginner in order to form a solid foundation in doing the right steps – from introductory concepts to making your first Day Trade.

Part Two is about Risk Management and what

Day Trading mistakes you can avoid in order to help minimize the chances of you losing your money. You'll learn how the process works and how to implement the steps discussed.

Part Three are the other important topics on Day Trading such as:

- Day Trading Tools
- Candlesticks – what it is, and it can help you in Day Trading
- Day Trading with Penny Stocks
- **BONUS Chapter:** Day Trading for Investors

Introduction:

Have you ever heard of "Day trading"? Well, "Options trading" maybe? If not, then do not worry, you've come to the right place - for I can assure you, I've taken care of all your needs within the pages of this book. I know the stock market can be intimidating! But, what can a person do if they want to improve their finances, manage their investments and create more wealth? This is where options trading or day trading comes in, and it is the solution you need!

However, the idea of making good money, as people know, always has risks involved, but in this case the risks are MINIMAL. Options trading, if used right, are bound to lead you to riches. Imagine your own yacht, or maybe even a private jet that's almost always up in the air flying you to all the places you've only dreamed of. Breakfasts near the Eiffel Tower and dinners in The Ritz-Carlton, perhaps? Well, you won't become successful overnight, but with preparation, determination and hard work, it sure can happen.

Now, that you've stumbled upon this book, you will get to learn the basics of options trading - what it is, and why you most definitely need it, the ideas and terms you'll need to be familiar with and need to know, along with the understanding of the various types of options, how to trade options, plan of action, the what to do and the what not to do - amongst various other things.

What good is any option without a cheat sheet that will aid you in making the ideal choice whilst investing? Well, a cheat sheet is exactly what I'll give you.

Many individuals, unfortunately, venture into the stock exchange without having any prior knowledge or information about what they're dealing with. This usually results in the person suffering from losses, which in turn leads to dissuasion from entering the stock market again. After he deals with one too many fruitless attempts, he starts to believe that making money with stock trading is just another publicity stunt, set to reel in hapless individuals.

For those who have wished to move into the trading world, but lack the finances or simply do not have the vital details necessary to start stock trading, they can begin with trading "options," using it as a stepping stone, before taking the big leap into the giant world of stock trading.

Many times, we come across a lot of information that talks about the "money" that a person can make by following a few simple steps. However, what these "information sources" fail to do is talk about the risks involved with this kind of trading. Therefore, it is highly recommended that you should get accustomed with the theory and acquire some background information before venturing into the market. In trading of stocks, you need to be watchful and wary. But you do not need to worry, it is not as difficult as it sounds and I will help you get the hang of how it works.

In this book, you will find information that will teach you how to understand the intricacies of day trading and unravel the mysteries associated with day trading. It will also elucidate on trading - options in particular. It will do this in such a way that you will not only get interested in trading but will also make you dig deeper and want to know more. So brace yourself and get ready to make that big leap into day trading.

I would like to take this opportunity to thank you for purchasing this book and I hope you find the information in this book useful.

Chapter 1: Trading & Investing Basics Explained

Chapter 1: Trading & Investing Basics Explained

What are Trading and Investing?

The two methods to make money in the business markets are trading and investing. The reason why someone invests is to accumulate wealth over a span of time, through the process of purchasing and holding a portfolio of bonds, shares, stocks, mutual funds and other investment options. Investors often try to increase their profits through a process called compounding or by reinvesting any profits they get in more shares and stocks. These investments are often held for long periods of time and these investors take advantage of the benefits of the stock exchange. It is a universally known fact that markets waver. In these cases, investors will overlook the downfalls with the belief that the prices will increase and that they will make up for their losses.

However, on the other hand, trading involves purchasing and selling stocks in a recurring pattern. Other items like commodities, currency pairs etc. are also bought with the aim of trading to make profits and to generate returns. Even though investors may be satisfied with a 15 to 20% annual return, traders tend to look for a 15% return every month. Profits are usually made in trading through buying low and selling high within a limited period of time.

So many different types of day trading patterns are available to traders today. Owing to the fact that there are so many options available today, some traders may get confused as to which trading technique is appropriate and more suitable for them.

In this section, you will be provided with an overview of the various types of trading.

Day Trading

As we have discussed above, the work of day traders is to purchase and sell their stocks within a single day hoping that the prices of their stocks will waver in rate throughout the day, resulting in them making huge profits. A Day Trader may hold onto a particular stock for a period of time, anywhere from a couple of seconds to a couple of hours. However, these traders will perpetually sell all their stocks prior to the closing of the market for that day. As the day trader doesn't possess any stock at the completion of any day he is unaffected by overnight changes or risks.

There are mainly two basic types of day trading; namely, Scalping and Momentum trading.

Scalping:

In this type of day trading, the trader repeatedly buys and sells a large volume of stocks within a very small amount of time, usually within seconds or minutes of purchasing them. The prime goal is to make a small profit per share on each transaction, whilst the overall financial risk is reduced.

Momentum Trading:

In this type of day trading, the trader identifies and trades stocks that seem to be moving in a pattern during the day. This way the trader tries to buy such stocks that are at the bottom and sell them when they reach the top. Thus, the trader makes a larger profit.

Swing Traders

Day trading differs from swing trading in the way that swing traders usually hold onto their stocks or positions for a more extended time period than day traders. Swing traders, also like day traders, try to foresee the interim fluctuations in the price of a stock. However, unlike day traders, swing traders are willing to hold onto their stocks for a time period of more than a day, if required. They do this if they feel the stock's price might move and if they believe they can make better profits based on this. Swing traders usually keep hold of their stock positions anywhere from a couple of hours to several days.

Position Trading

Position trading is comparable to swing trading. However, position trading has a longer trading period. In Position trading, the traders hold onto their stocks for a period of time anywhere from a day to many weeks or even many months at a stretch. These traders try to look out for stocks where the trends seem to suggest that there might be a large change in the price of that stock. This change in price may not happen for many weeks or even months.

Online Trading

Online trading isn't usually mentioned as a type of trading. Instead, online trading is mainly a term that denotes the medium that is utilized to enter the stock exchange and execute trades. Online traders, which include investors, who have been in the stock exchange for a long time, swing, day and position traders, utilize the Internet or an online trading platform that they use to directly access the stock market and to perform trades with brokers who are based online.

A Brief History of Trading

In the U.S., securities markets started with

speculative trading concerning issues of the new government. The U.S.A's first stock exchange was set up in Philadelphia in 1791, because Philadelphia was the then leading city in domestic and foreign trade. In New York, an exchange was established in 1792, when 24 merchants and brokers resolved to charge commissions, while they acted as agents for other persons, and gave priority to each other in their negotiations. Most of their trading was done under a tree at 68 Wall Street.

Thus, these government securities created the basis of the early trading. Stocks of banks and insurance companies supplemented their other transactions. With the building of canals and roads, more securities were brought to the market. These New York brokers decided to get together formally as the New York Stock and Exchange Board in 1817. Soon after, the stock market grew during the country's Industrialization era. The New York Stock Exchange took up its present name in 1863. More exchanges were organized during the Civil War; one of them was the precursor of the current American Stock Exchange. It was the second largest stock market in the country for a long time.

The need to learn the basics of trading:

When a person decides to take the first step in a new direction, it is necessary to take that first step with some prior knowledge. There are risks associated with any investment. There is no gain without a touch of risk. For this reason, it is necessary to learn the basics of trading and this book will help you in doing just that. By the time you finish this book, you'll know the basics of trading and how to go about trading to become a successful trader. By learning the basics

- You will not require a broker and will be able to make your own investments.
- You will be able to accurately gauge whether the market looks positive or negative and with that knowledge you can either buy or sell your stocks accordingly.
- You will learn to observe the trends and that will influence the investments you make.
- You will understand not to gamble with more than 5% of your total investment on just one trade.
- You will realize that you need to be levelheaded and not give into greed or fear or follow the herd mentality.

This is just some of the knowledge that you will gain when you learn the basics of trading.

How basic trading is done:

There are two Basic Methods:

- On the New York Stock Exchange floor
- Through Electronic means

New York Stock Exchange Floor

Owing to television and movies, we all have an image of trading that happens on the New York Stock Exchange floor.

Do you recall that moment when the market opens? Hundreds of people are running about and yelling, signaling to each other, taking calls while looking at monitors, and recording data into their terminals. There is absolute chaos all around.

Here is a step-by-step procedure of the completion of a basic trade on the floor of the NYSE.

- Firstly you tell your broker which shares you want to buy and how many.
- The floor clerk receives an order from your broker about the exchange.
- The floor clerk signals one of the firm's traders who work on the floor, this person then locates another trader who works on the floor who is ready to sell the shares you wish to buy.
- Both of them decide on a value and the deal is completed. The announcement course goes back up along the same line

and then you receive a call from your broker who gives you the last price. This procedure might take a couple of minutes or even longer depending on the market and the stock. After a few days, you will get the news of confirmation by mail.

This is an example of a simple trade. Complex trades and big chunks of stocks include more steps and details.

Through Electronic Means

In this electronically advanced and fast-paced world, people sometimes wonder as to how much longer a human-based system. For instance, the NYSE, can go on to supply the service required. The NYSE manages a minuscule percentage of its stock exchanges electronically. NASDAQ, its rival, manages all of its exchanges electronically.

These electronic stock markets make use of assessing and extensive computer networks to pair sellers and buyers online without the use of human brokers.

As an investor, you can often get risk confirmation of your trades most of the time. It also simplifies the process by investing online and puts you one step closer to the market. However, you still require a broker to take care of your trades – private individuals do not have a means of entry to these electronic markets. Your middleman finds you a suitable buyer or seller based on your requirements.

Chapter Summary:

1. In this chapter, you were provided with an introduction to trading and investment, the history of trading and the different types of trading.
2. Using this knowledge you can easily decide which trading method best suits you.
3. You were also provided with the reasons why you should read up on the basics of trading and the benefits associated with it.
4. In addition, this chapter also provided you with a step-by-step procedure of how trading happens and what to expect out of it.

Without further ado, let's delve into the next chapter and focus on what Day Trading is and how to become a successful day trader.

Your Quick Start Action Steps:

In this first Action Step, you can go check out this website and gain a greater insight into what investing candlesticks and trading is for beginners. Hope you find it informative and useful.

http://www.businessnewsdaily.com/4508-online-trading.html

Chapter 2: Day Trading Essentials

Chapter 2: Day Trading Essentials

If you do not want your money to just lie around and you are looking for places to invest your money, you've come to the right place. There are various options available to invest in, like mutual funds, stocks, bonds etc. In addition to these usual and traditional investment options, there is another upcoming and impressive way to trade called 'Day Trading' or 'Trading Options.' This way, making money through trading is very flexible. The process of selling and buying stocks in the period of a single day is called Day trading. In Day Trading, individuals try to make profits by using large capital to make use of small changes in the price of indexes or liquid stocks. Individuals who involve themselves in day trading are called day traders.

As a beginner day trader, there is a lot that you need to learn. Day Trading is risky, especially if not done with sufficient knowledge. But do not worry; with the help of this book, you can become a financially savvy Day Trader in no time at all.

Day Trading, at one point of time, was exclusively done only by financial firms and professional speculators. However, today even private individuals like you and me can do Day

Trading. With the kind of flexibility that day trading offers, users can make changes anytime during the trading process. The trader can either choose to be extremely cautious and careful or can choose to jump into the risky end-trading spectrum, where they could either make a very large profit or make a huge loss. It is a well-established fact that no investment is safe from loss. However, there are certain investments that give you a better profit with only marginal risk factors. Though options help you make more profits, they have as much higher risk associated with them as bonds and mutual funds do.

Now that we know what options are, we are also interested in trading options. Let's try to explain the different types of options and find out which option is a better choice.

Binary Options are of 2 types, they are:

1. Call Option
2. Put Option

Fundamentally, a 'call option' allows you to buy at a given price for a particular time period. These individuals, who buy call options are hopeful that the stock prices will rise, and that they can make a better profit before the stocks perish.

Some important guidelines that need to be met for an option to be a "call option" are:

1. The underlying stock or index
2. The option must have an expiry date
3. The strike price of the option
4. The option gives the "right to BUY" a stock/index.

To get a more profound understanding of the call and put options, it is essential to understand a few basic slangs and the candlestick process involved.

Let's take the example of a stock B which is priced at $15, and you as a trader expect the stock to at least go up by a $1 and end at $16 – which is called "strike price" before the deal closes for the stock in say a few weeks.

Because you expect the price to go up by $1, the actual price that you'll be paying to make the trade is $1.00; this is the price of your deal/ option.

This means, if the stock price reaches $16, you will break even and make a profit, even if the stock goes up a few cents beyond $16 in those couple of weeks, or else you might be at a loss, and, in this case, you will lose $1 per call option. The difference between the strike price ($16) that you predicted and the actual price that the stock rose to or fell to is the value of a call option.

If we presume that the stock price went up to $25 at the end of 2 weeks, the value of call option is $9 and that's also the profit that you make per call option.

However, if the stock price goes down to $10 at the end of 2 weeks, which is the specified time, then it will end up in a loss. However, you will be able to tell whether there will be an increase or a decrease based on speculation. Most people don't care about small losses, especially in the beginning, as it helps them to learn and work the market better. The next time that they decide to invest, they will be much more careful and know where to and where not to invest their money.

The second type of option that we are going to talk about is called the 'put' options or "exotic" options. This option gives the buyer the option to barter a financial resource at strike price before a definite expiry time. In "put options" the scenario is comparable to having the power to take a short decision on stocks while trading. By selling the stock at a predicted strike price, put options allow you to make money. Here, the profit is made when the stocks lose money; thus it is riskier and is an interesting trade option. For put options, experience is required. Buyers of put options hope that the price of a stock whose options they hold actually will reduce by x amount before the close of business so that they can make some money.

So, let us assume that a stock C is currently

priced at $20. You then speculate and predict, based on a number of parameters, that the price is most likely to fall by $1, you pay a price of $2 to buy the stock which will expire in say 2 weeks, during which period the profit that one makes is limited by the following formula,

Max Profit = $21 - $2

= $19

In this stock option, the profit that one can make is limited.

It is preferable to try and break even if it is not possible to make a profit. This is true for both cases. Well-established options will ensure that you do not undergo a loss and will earn back the cash that you put in. It will also save you from feeling guilty for choosing the wrong type of option. Although it isn't seen that one option is better than the other, some people prefer the put option as there is no time frame as such and it will be easier for him or her to trade. But, there are also those who prefer the call option. The decision is entirely up to you.

That is the type of stock option available in the market for trading; now it is time to understand the various players in the day trading market.

Day Trading has been in practice for more than a century. Today, we have electronics to help us, but the idea of buying and selling stocks by the public dates back to the late 19th century. During this time, small businesses were set up in major cities across the United States where people could opt to go to make "plays" in the market. These businesses were called as "bucket shops." The players would all donate money into the common "bucket." This money then gets utilized as reassurance for buying stocks or such commodities. This practice allowed the small time traders to consider stocks that would have otherwise been out of their reach. People made profits or lost their money based on how fundamentally honest the shop operators were. Without a doubt, most of these shops were illegitimate and illegal. With the 1929 Stock Market Crash, these shops were shut down and went out of existence.

The importance of learning the basics of Day Trading:

There are facts and rules about day trading that all people who are going to try their hand at day trading should be aware of. The major reason why some traders lose money with either stocks, currencies, or anything else, is because they do not seem to possess a basic understanding of important concepts like these. Don't be a victim like them. Even though these rules sound easy and simplistic, they are vital and necessary and adherence to these rules is a must.

- If the market looks positive – going up, either sell your put options or buy call options. However, if you sense that the market is going down, do the opposite – sell calls, buy puts. Selling is a better strategy than buying. You might end up making quite a profit. However, you must be able to sense which ones will bring the highest profits when sold. A friend who deals in stocks and shares could provide you with advice. Once you get the hang of it, you will be able to sell with confidence.
- Always remember to let the first hour of the day pass by without any trading from your end. After that, make note if the stock's price, the one that you are interested in is going in the same direction as it was in the morning and if it's good, then make an "at the market" buy.
- Don't ever forget to observe the trend and make wise and calculated decisions.

These are just some of the things that you need to keep in mind. Once you gain an in-depth understanding of day trading, there will be so much more that you will discover.

General Steps Involved in Day Trading:

Now we seem to know what Day Trading is. We know what the other types of trading are. Now, let's get to the action. Here are the various processes involved in Day Trading.

Pay attention and read it carefully as it is essential if you plan to be a day trader.

Get a Laptop

The basic necessity for day trading is a laptop for your personal use. You will have to devote an entire computer system to day trading, as you will have to keep an eye on the markets the entire time. If you happen to be using the computer for some other purpose, then you might end up missing a good deal.

Internet Connection

The next essential item is a good Internet connection. As you already know, day trading requires that you look at the prices of stocks on a minute-to-minute basis and that can only be done with the help of a fast and efficient Internet connection

Opening an Account

The next thing you are expected to do is to open a trading account with a company. The trading company you open an account with should be well reputed and should help you trade smoothly. Remember to read reviews about the trading company before you open an account with them.

Installment of Software

The next thing to do is to install the required software. Software refers to the one that you will be utilizing to engage in day trading. The trading company will provide you with the software and will also help you install it.

Employing a Broker

This broker will help you buy and sell the shares. But you can choose either to work with a broker or work independently. Just remember to employ a day trading broker, especially when you are just starting out so that they can help you with the basics.

Knowledge

The next thing to do is to gain the knowledge necessary for carrying out day-to-day trades in the market. This book can help you in your journey no doubt, but you must not limit yourself to what is provided in this book. You should try to acquire as much knowledge as you can to equip yourself with the skills required to be a successful trader.

Research

You must do a small amount of research on the market trends before investing. This will make sure that you make the correct investment decisions.

Budget

It is essential to set a budget for yourself if you want to trade wisely. Your budget should be according to your spending capacity and the amount of money that you can afford to invest.

Buy stocks

The next thing to do is to purchase the stocks. These stocks are to be bought from the stock market and you should possess a good variety of stocks, to begin with.

Keep a Watch List

A watch list will be useful when you want to keep track of the various stocks that you own. A watch list is meant to learn about the different stocks so that you will know when the right time to sell them is.

Sell your stocks

The next obvious step is the selling of your stocks. You have to make a profit and the only way you can do so is by selling whatever you own. But make sure that you sell your stocks when the price is high.

Repeat the steps

The final thing to do is to repeat all the above steps, again. Thus, begin by buying stocks, hold them and then sell them. You will need to do this on an everyday basis if you want to be a day trader.

Chapter Summary:

1. In this chapter, you were provided with an introduction to day trading and the history of day trading
2. This chapter also contained the reasons of why it is necessary to learn the basics of day trading and how this can help a person be successful. It also contained the various benefits of equipping yourself with basic knowledge
3. Finally, there are the general steps involved in Day Trading and the methods that should be employed to become a day trader.

Your Quick Start Action Steps:

In this second Action Step, you can go check out this website and gain a greater insight into day trading for beginners. We've all got to start somewhere.

http://www.tradingacademy.com/resources/financial-education-center/10-day-trading-secrets-for-beginners.aspx

Chapter 3:
The Benefits Of
Day Trading

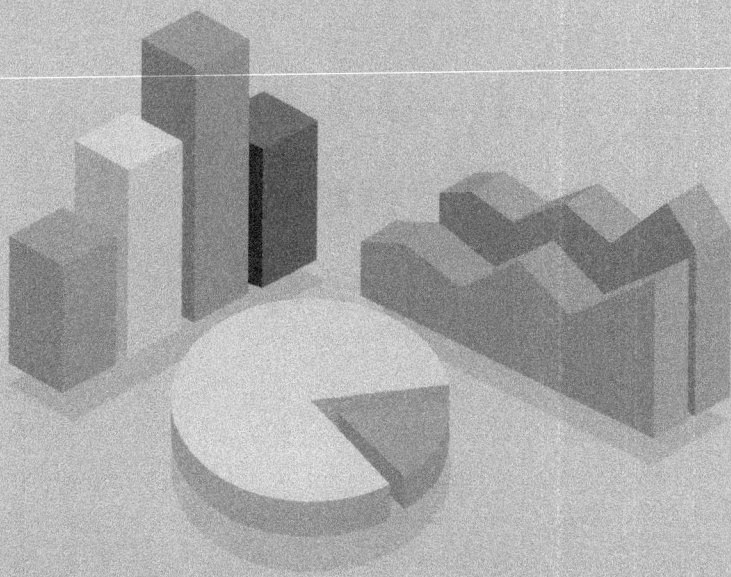

Chapter 3: The Benefits Of Day Trading

Importance of understanding the benefits:

You need to be interested in gathering information that is absolutely essential for your investment. Your investment will only be successful if you put in the required effort and understand the benefits of day trading and the risk factors associated with it. No one is saying that you need to stay up all night and go through thick, fat textbooks. All you have to do is go through certain books (such as this one!) and websites to gather enough information to help you get started. Once you are confident that you have gathered sufficient information you can start your Day Trading journey.

- You should always do a thorough research of the market before you start investing in it. Learning as you go isn't an option here. You can only learn as you go once you know the processes that are involved.
- You should not care about message boards. These boards will be available on the Internet and mostly help people to gather information. However, there

will be pumpers and bashers present on these boards. People will be forced to buy a stock just to increase its value and also will be forced to sell all their stocks just because the value should go down. Both these types of transactions are risky and you should be very careful while dealing with them.

- You will learn to not buy something just because it's cheap. This temptation to buy something that isn't needed just because it's available at a cheaper price is a huge mistake that a trader must avoid – this is popularly known as "The Price Tag problem"

How do you stay focused on Day Trading?

It is believed that focus is extremely important and it can make or break your Day Trading Career. To become a successful trader it is extremely important to concentrate on your work and not get distracted. Here are some strategies to remain focused:

1. Do not spend more than 2 to 3 hours per day doing Day Trading. The longer you work, the likelier it is that you will get distracted. This focus doesn't happen overnight and requires practice and patience.

2. Remember to keep your watch list small. If you have 5 solid plays per day that's enough to keep you going.
3. Focus on your strengths and skills and design an appropriate trading strategy. Don't try to do more than you can. You'll overwork yourself and miss out.
4. Just focus on your own intuitions and beliefs. That will help you trade better. You need to figure out which kinds of messages actually aid your trading strategy and which ones just confuse you.
5. Make sure you eliminate distractions and focus only on your trading during this designated work time. No messy desks, no social media breaks and so on.

Chapter Summary:

1. In this chapter, we focused on the benefits and the risks associated with day trading
2. It explained the reasons as to why it is so important to learn about day trading if a person wants to make a hobby or a career out of it.
3. The chapter also contains strategies to help a person to focus on day trading to become a better day trader.

Your Quick Start Action Step:

In addition to the information provided here,

please read up as much as you can online and access different websites to equip yourself with more knowledge. Day Trading cannot be learned in a day and requires focus and dedication. These websites will help you understand that better.

http://www.investopedia.com/articles/trading /o6/daytradingretail.asp

http://humbletraders.com/day-trading-strategies/

Chapter 4:
Day Trading
Success

Chapter 4: Day Trading Success

Who is a successful day trader?

As the saying goes "Rome wasn't built in a day."

Success doesn't happen overnight. To become successful in trading it'll take time and practice. No one can make successful investments by playing it safe all the time. However, a person can be wary and careful and assess the risks and watch out for whether the profits outweigh the risks. This can only be done if a person has a basic understanding of what he is getting himself into.

It has been found that the success rate of day traders is about 10% - if that's true, then about 90% are losing money, then how can anyone expect to make a living this way? It is all possible with training, earnest research, skills that are polished, discipline and the ability to own up to mistakes. You should always be ready to make split-second, unbiased and unemotional decisions based on information that sometimes seems incomplete, conflicting and uncertain. This is clearly easier said than done. But don't worry, day trading can be enjoyable and can help you make big bucks. All you need to do is to learn the ropes of the trade and set achievable goals.

Day Trading does have potentially enormous profits if done successfully. Added to these advantages are benefits for some rare people who can manage their emotions and withstand the pressures associated with Day Trading. They are:

Independence.

Day traders, more often than not, are self-employed individuals, who work as their own boss and are not answerable to anyone. Their craft is their business and they are free to make their own decisions and are directly responsible for the success or failure on a daily basis.

Euphoria.

When you get the financial success and earn profits on decisions taken on your own terms, it gives you a great emotional high. This feeling of euphoria can rarely be matched by any other, especially when it comes to professional successes.

Status.

Being a Day traders counts as a highly regarded job in certain communities, as they make money on their own terms.

Parameters of successful day trading

Before you decide to make a career or hobby out of this you need to be educated and informed about the arena you are venturing into. People come to realize that day trading is one of the toughest ways to make easy cash.

Here are some parameters of successful trading:

- Successful traders remain emotionally detached and are able to make neutral decisions about their trades.
- Successful traders do not allow their fear to overpower them. They are confident of their decisions.
- Successful day traders only use capital that they can afford to risk and are thus, able to take neutral decisions.
- Successful day traders don't take up every strategy that comes their way but focus on certain strategies that they know suit them well.
- Don't worry, you will make mistakes, but don't lose hope. The day traders who are extremely patient are most successful.

- Successful day traders know how to effectively manage their money. He won't be willing to lose more than 2% of his capital in any trade.
- Successful day traders excel at their work because they trade with confidence.

Measuring the success of day trading

The job of a day trader is to buy and sell securities, repeatedly during the day, but it also entails selling off all his stock before the market closes for the day.

- A good Day trader knows how to control his emotions and stays composed at all times.
- If he makes a mistake, he does not personalize the loss, but just goes on and tries harder the next day. Traders who are successful are aware that losses are bound to happen.
- A trader's psychological take on the situation, like a loss, determines how successful he or she will be.
- It needs to be understood that this is not the solution to get rich quickly and requires time and effort.
- How hardworking and committed an individual determines how successful he

will be.

- To be a successful day trader one also requires working capital. Day trading is like any other business. You need to put in money to make more money.

Chapter Summary:

1. In this chapter, we saw the basis of who is a successful day trader and what makes him / her successful.
2. The parameters of successful day trading were discussed.
3. We also saw the steps using which one can measure how successful they can be as a day trader and what they can improve to become better day traders.

Your Quick Start Action Step:

In this chapter, we advised you to go online and read up about successful day traders and to make note of their advice and the tips that they offer. I hope that helps you.

Chapter 5:
Making Your First
Day Trade

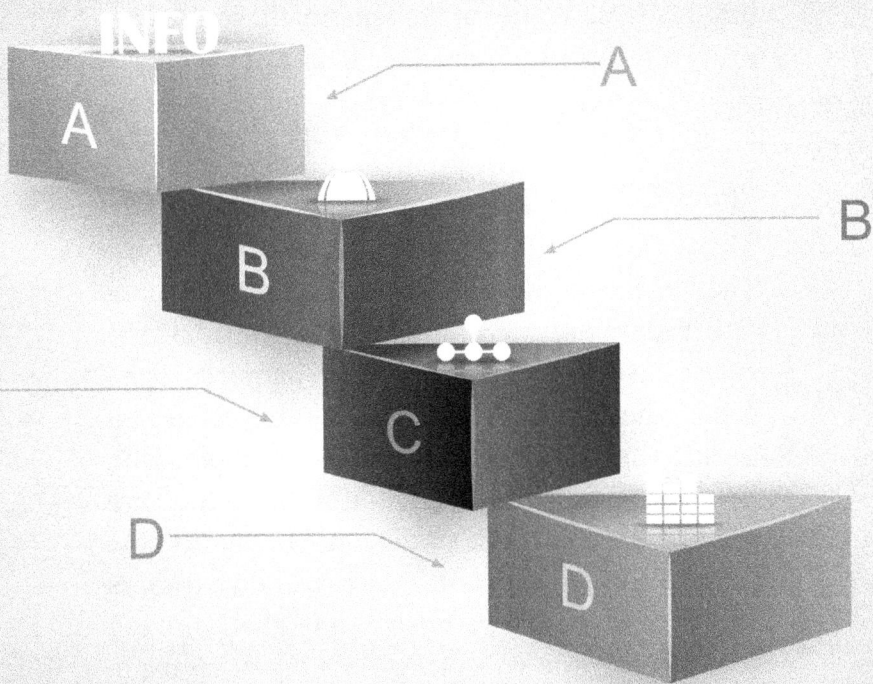

Chapter 5: Making Your First Day Trade

Aspects of Day Trading:

There are various characteristics that make a successful day trader. In this section, I shall list some aspects that are common to successful day traders. You can implement these aspects into your lives and become a better day trader.

They have a controlled and disciplined approach.

These people don't trade just on "intuition." They back their hunches with hard data. These day traders are successful because they develop rules based on the data they acquire. They utilize these rules while trading. They plan and decide the amount of money in their portfolio they want to risk, the amount that they are ready to lose on each trade, and when and how they will make a profit. Successful day traders will formulate rules and be controlled enough to adhere to the rules they set - on every trade they take up.

Their risk taking abilities

In general, day traders take a lot of risks. This fact is absolutely certain. But even though they do take risks they aren't reckless or careless. Rather these people take calculated risks that favor them. It's important to remember the old saying, "Without risk, there is no reward." Investing in stock is an intrinsically risky venture, but in day trading the risk is multifold. Hence, if you want to get deep into day trading you must be ready to take risks and accept the consequences that come with those risks.

They are patient and determined

Day trading, like any other job, takes time and effort for you to become good at. Day traders, in general, are bound to make losses initially, and a lot of people just give up when they experience their first loss. However, day traders who are good at what they do will continue doing trade use their mistakes as lessons. This will eventually lead to them making a profit. Profits and losses are bound to happen. What is crucial is that you don't give up and instead learn from your losses.

They effectively cope with Stress

Wherever there is a high chance of losing money, there is bound to be stress. Hence, every day the market is open, a day trader has to face stress. Coping with stress effectively and not letting it interfere with your trading strategy is extremely important if you want to be a profitable day trader.

They have good control over their emotions

Day traders who are successful operate based on a fixed set of practices that are based on numbers, analytics and math. They should be willing to put the effort to keep their emotions in check. It really doesn't matter whether or not they like a company, they will have to isolate their true feelings towards the company from the strategies they use in trading. Successful day traders don't spend too much time and effort worrying about the bottom line or fundamentals of a company. They invest more time in gaining knowledge about the everyday technical indicators of the company they are interested in. In essence, they will have to be ready to purchase a company that isn't making a profit on an upswing and sell a company that is profitable on a downswing.

Decision-making skills

Day traders need to have the ability to make quick and smart decisions. Delaying selling or buying an order can result in loss of profits. Therefore, the capability to make any decision at a moment's notice is one of the most important characteristics of a successful day trader.

Why these steps are crucial for

success:

Though one can make a lot of money by being a day trader, a large number of people who try their hand at day trading aren't all that successful. Being a successful day trader doesn't have much to do the availability of capital, but has much more to do with individual character traits. If you feel you don't possess the aforementioned characteristics, but still want to day trade, then it is of great importance that you cultivate these traits. Without these traits, you will not be able to be a successful day trader.

It is extremely important to follow these steps to make money and be financially independent, that's what most of us are aiming for. However, you should also understand that life needs to be enjoyed and we needn't suffer in the name of making money. Make your money, but at the same time remember to live life to the fullest. Go to the gym, go have coffee with your friends, and don't just sit in front of the trading screen all day.

What knowing the steps will do:

- You will take the first step on the path towards becoming a successful day trader.
- It will make you feel confident and financially independent

- You will learn to control your emotions in other aspects of life as well
- This focus that you learn can be applied to other spheres of your life
- You will be able to face both profits and losses and take it all in your stride.

Steps involved in basic day trading:

In chapter 2, we already saw the basic steps involved in day trading. I am sure you have gained more knowledge with respect to this subject. With that in mind let's have a more detailed look at the steps involved in day trading. With the aid of these steps, you can go about and start day trading with confidence.

Buy a Computer

First and foremost you will have to buy yourself a computer. Most of us already have a computer, but you will require another one to conduct your trade operations. Don't make the mistake of using just one computer for all your work. You might get confused and your work might get mixed up. We don't want that now, do we? Make it a point to have two separate workstations, one for your regular work and one for trading. If possible, try setting up an office at home as this will motivate you. Also, make sure that there are not too many things around you that could distract you.

Seek Knowledge

The next step is to gain as much knowledge as you can on the subject. By now you would have a basic knowledge of what day trading is, however, it is essential that you gain more knowledge about this subject. Try to read as much as you can, whenever possible. Make sure to learn about how risk is calculated and if you are a good candidate for day trading or not. You can read from the websites that I have provided and also purchase more books that can educate you more on this specific subject. Once you feel that you have gained enough knowledge, move on to the next step.

Website registration

It is of extreme importance that you register with a company where you can sell and buy stocks. There are many companies that you can choose from, so choose the company that best suits you. Once you're done registering, they will help you download the software that you will need to buy and sell stocks. You require a special software for this purpose and this software is only available with these websites that trade stocks. Using this software you can look at the stocks that are up for sale and you can click on them to either buy or sell them. These software's are mostly downloaded onto your computer, but some companies may also send across their technicians to help you download and install the software onto your computer. After the software is up and running, you can start trading. Just consider the next step before you start trading.

Preparing the Mind

It is very important to mentally prepare yourself before you start day trading. You need to understand that day trading is an uncertain trade and that you must mentally prepare yourself for both profits and losses. You should always keep your cool and shouldn't make rash or hasty decisions. It is normal to get angry and be upset at times, but you should keep your calm despite all these emotions while you are trading. You need to remain alert and should not be distracted by anything. Make sure you are hydrated and your energy is at its peak as you will be required to use your brain a lot while trading.

Observe and pay close attention

The next thing to do is to become acquainted with the software that you will be making use of for your trading. You need to know everything about your software, including its operation and the way it works. If you start trading without learning and comprehending the basics, you will find it difficult to trade. Next, always keep a watch out for the trends in the market. Remember to look for the stocks that are doing well or ones that you believe have potential. Every stock or security tends to have a graph and these graphs give you an idea of how it has been doing so far. From analyzing these graphs you will have an idea as to whether this stock is good and with that opinion in mind you can either decide to invest in that stock or not invest in it.

Brokerage

As an amateur day trader, you will often start to feel overwhelmed and not know where to start or what to do. This is particularly true for beginners as they are new to this and won't know where to start trading. If after consecutive attempts you still cannot seem to comprehend what is the best option for you then you can consider consulting a broker.

As it was previously explained, brokers are middlemen who will help you to invest money in the stock exchange. You can hire a broker at any time and their job is to help you out. You can set up a brokerage account after contacting a broker. After this, you transfer your money and ask them to help you in learning the ins and outs of investing. Once they trade a couple of stocks for you, you will have a better idea of the working of the market and gain the confidence to do it on your own.

Buy

The next step is to buy the stocks. When buying

stocks, remember to buy stocks or securities in bulk. It won't be possible to buy one or two stocks at a time. In addition, next to the stock value there will be a minimum amount that you are required to purchase. This minimum value differs from company to company. It also differs from Website to Website and hence, you must pay attention to the minimum amount that one needs to invest in order to buy stocks for day trading purposes. If on the other hand, you opt for options, you will be expected to pay an advance towards the stocks or securities that you want to reserve.

Wait

Once the stocks have been purchased, you are advised to wait. Keep in mind what I told you earlier about letting the first hour pass. After this time, you will have a clearer idea of which direction the stocks are heading in. If you believe that the stocks are rising then that's good for you. However, if you feel that they are falling then don't start worrying as they might rise again by the end of the trading day. Make sure you are paying close attention to the market trends. You will have to do this regularly. People who take up day trading as their main job are usually expected to spend time in front of their computers and pay attention to the trends throughout the day. They are expected to pay close attention till the trade closes for the day. If you even have the slightest thought that you won't be able to do this then consider hiring a broker to help you.

Sell

The following step is to sell all your securities and stocks. This needs to be done before the market closes for the day. Selling is also called as liquidating and for options, it is called as "liquidating your position." Keep in mind that you will have to sell all your stock within the same day for it to be regarded as day trading. If you don't sell your stock and hold it overnight then it will be known as regular trading. By selling it you will have the chance to make a profit. Your profit will be subtracted from the value of your purchased stock and this profit will be transferred to your account. Always remember that you have to make wise investment decisions. Also, see that you are earning a good profit before you buy and sell stocks and securities.

Maintain Records

You should always keep a record of your transactions. These records need to be in detail. You will require these records for future reference. If possible try to maintain both soft and hard copies. With the help of a detailed report, you can measure your profits and losses and this provides you with an opportunity to predict a pattern. You can follow this pattern while selling and buying stocks. It is recommended that by the time the month ends, you look through the entire month's data and analyze it.

Repeat

Well, now we've come to the last step in this process. Once you believe that you have gotten the hang of day trading. Just repeat the process and do what works best for you. By doing this you will fall into the pattern of buying stocks later selling them and then recording the data. After some time, this will come to you naturally and you will be setting yourself up for a successful career in day trading. But, always keep in mind that you need to stay cautious and only engage in activities that you feel are beneficial to you.

To get started on your day trading activities you can adopt these various steps. But, also keep in mind that these are just suggestions and you need to follow what works best for you.

Chapter Summary:

1. In this chapter, you were shown the different aspects and characteristics of day traders and day trading.
2. You also learned about why it is absolutely essential to follow these steps required to become a successful day trader.
3. In the last part of this chapter, the steps

involved in day trading were explained in great detail, along with, what an individual needs to do to take up day trading.

Your Quick Start Action Step:

In this chapter, I suggested that you take some time out of your schedule and try to implement the steps mentioned in the previous section (5.3)

Chapter 6:
Day Trading
Mistakes:
What To Avoid

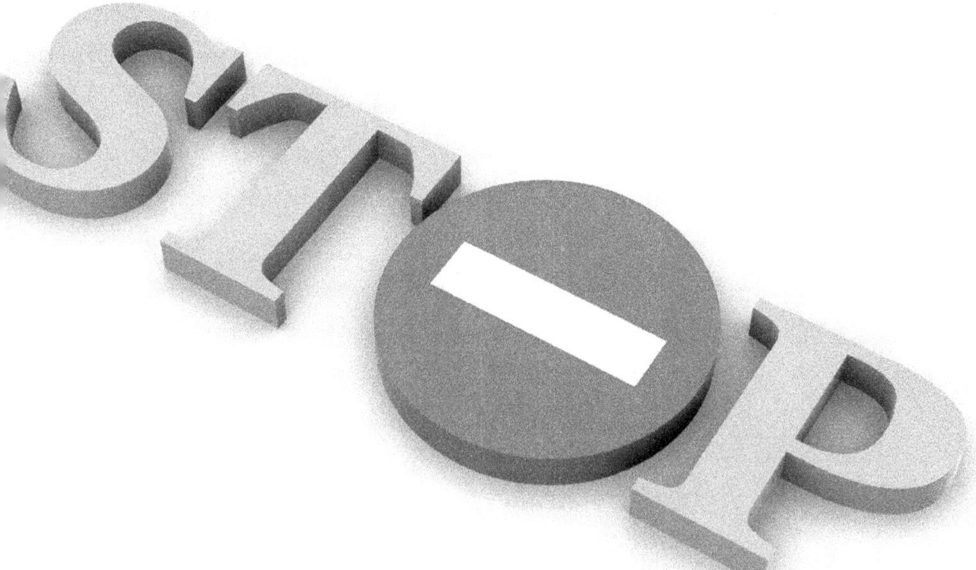
STOP

Chapter 6: Day Trading Mistakes: What To Avoid

Traders, in general, tend to sell and buy securities more often and hold their positions for a lesser period of time than investors. As a result of such recurrent trading and shorter holding periods, new traders can make mistakes that are detrimental to their success. It is important to remember that, when it comes to day trading, there are certain mistakes that one can make. Some of these mistakes are listed below:

- I have done much research and have gotten most of my information from authentic sources like: The Worst Mistakes Beginner Traders Make | Investopedia http://www.investopedia.com/articles/active-trading/013015/worst-mistakes-beginner-traders-make.asp#ixzz4e9fKMSAR
- Day Trading: Beginners Guild to Building Riches through the Stock - By James Carnegie

Financial mistakes:

These mistakes should be the first thing you consider when you have decided to start day trading. Please pay close attention to these mistakes before the start of your journey.

Don't invest too much

Keep in mind that you should not take a chance with a lot of your money. The day trading market is very uncertain and unpredictable. Even with a lot of research, the market trends are difficult to predict. The price of your stock may fluctuate during the day and you might end up losing money in the end. For this reason, you need to be careful about how much money you invest into it. As a rule of thumb, keep it a point to invest a particular amount of money every day and don't invest an excess amount of money into your stocks. Make sure you settle on a particular amount and invest only that much money every day.

Remember not to expect too much

Success doesn't happen overnight so it's a smart decision to keep your expectations low. This means that you should not expect to make huge profits within a brief period of time. It is not possible for you to become a millionaire overnight. Day Trading does not work that way. The markets could be unstable and you won't be able to make a big profit overnight. It may take a couple of months or years before you begin to make a consistent profit. Until that time you should remain focused and consistent.

Keep track of your losses

You always need to factor in your losses. It is impossible to trade without facing losses along the way. Remember that you always need to consider your losses if you are planning to start day trading. It is a known fact that the share market is extremely volatile and fickle. If you don't accept your losses and take them in your stride then you might get into problems. Always play close attention to your monthly graphs and know the number of times you have lost money. Once this task is done try to work on your investment plan to make it more successful. But beware, it is impossible to eliminate all losses in your trade, as it is practically impossible to have a constant winning streak.

Herd Mentality

A very common mistake that new traders make is to blindly follow the herd. As a result of this mentality, they pay way too much money for their stocks and losing while selling. As mentioned earlier, to be successful in trading, one mustn't give into fear and greed. While traders, who have been trading for some time now, are experienced and seem to follow the market trends, they know the tricks when entering a trade and when to exit it. New traders, on the other hand, may continue investing in the stocks even after the money has moved out of those stocks.

"Be fearful when others are greedy and greedy only when others are fearful."- Warren Buffet

Mistakes regarding career

Here are some errors of judgment that you might encounter while doing day trading. These mistakes are with respect to your career.

Don't take it up as your main job

Day trading cannot be taken up as the main job. This is particularly true if you are just starting to day trade. Do not make the rash decision of quitting your day job just because you have decided to take up day trading. It is important to have a consistent source of income until you become a well established and successful day trader. It is impossible to predict how much time it will take. For some people, it may even take a couple of years. Even if you find yourself making profits once you start trading, patience and consistency are key. See if you continue to make similar profits later on. Once you feel you have learned it all and you are confident, you can make the choice to become a full-time day trader

Use it as a parallel source of income

In addition to your active income, you could have a portfolio income as well. But for this, you need to be serious about day trading. You should not be among those who take it nonchalantly and invest in day trading just to pass their time. If you take up day trading as a pastime, it'll cause you to suffer losses. So take day trading seriously and it can become a good alternate source of income.

Productivity

One fact that usually bothers most day traders is the number of hours they need to spend staring at a computer screen to make the best deals and follow the trends. This worry will cause them to waste a lot of their time. In the end that will be unproductive. Owing to this fact they may miss out on many good opportunities. Hence, it is advised for people to take up day trading in their spare time. If you are enthusiastic about taking up day trading while at work, then the best option for you is to consider hiring a discounted broker who will help you. After following the trends if you see an opportunity, you can give him a call and ask him to buy or sell the stock.

Social life

Just as people worry about being unproductive while taking up day trading, they also worry about losing out on their social lives. For this reason, it is important that you engage in day trading as and when you get free time and don't settle for less in your social life. If you decide to take a couple of days off socializing, you can get back to day trading anytime. Remember to take time out for yourself and once in a while splurge on yourself and pamper yourself.

Mistakes concerning one's health:

Just like one can make mistakes in one's finances and career, there are mistakes concerning health that you should pay attention to.

Mental strength

In day trading you are expected to think a lot and this can cause mental exhaustion. For this reason, you should try to be as mentally strong as possible. You can do this with the help of mind games that keep you fresh and your brain active. Try your hand at games like chess to strengthen your mental ability. If you feel it is too much and you feel overwhelmed then consider taking a break and maybe take a walk around the park to refresh your mind.

Emotional support

Initially, you will be extremely enthusiastic and will be highly motivated. But, as time goes by, you'll start to realize that these activities are both physically and emotionally draining. You will have to look after your finances, you will need to dedicate time to the needs of your family, etc. and all of it might start to feel so overpowering that you may consider giving up. To tackle this issue, you will require emotional support from your family and friends. Understand they will be by your side irrespective of whether you are making a profit or a loss.

Need to avoid these mistakes:

Always keep in mind that day trading is only meant to be a parallel source of income and an investment, which will help you safeguard your future. Don't worry, these mistakes are mentioned just for precaution and are not meant to discourage you from taking up day trading. It is better to be safe than sorry. Day trading is a great opportunity for both novice and experienced investors and it will help you to diversify your investment options. If you keep track of these mistakes and watch out for them then you can hope for a bright future in day trading. People who follow these rules can expect the following:

- Their trading will become a profitable venture.
- They will know that they can depend on their friends and family.
- They will realize how important it is to take time out for oneself.
- They will make it a point to enjoy life to the fullest
- They will find that day trading is an

amazing way to supplement one's income.

Steps to avoid these mistakes:

1. As the saying goes 'When the going gets tough, the tough get going'. You need to remain persistent and make smart business decisions.
2. You should be cautious of stocks and securities that you feel will end up causing losses for you and you should try to avoid investing in them.
3. Try to remain calm and composed at all times.
4. Day trading is just a part of your life. Don't take it up so seriously that it overwhelms you.
5. Take days off, go on a vacation. Remember to relax and have fun.
6. It has been proven that playing with children and pets reduces stress and pressure. Try doing whatever works best for you and always keep your calm.

Chapter Summary:

1. In this chapter, I have covered the mistakes that one should avoid while day trading.
2. The need to avoid these mistakes and the benefits that come with that are also explained in great detail.
3. The steps that people can take up to

avoid making these mistakes have also been listed in this chapter.

Your Quick Start Action Step:

In this chapter, I urge you to play close attention to these mistakes and avoid them when you make your next day trade.

Chapter 7:
Day Trading Risk
Management

Chapter 7: Day Trading Risk Management

What is risk management?

Risk management is when you identify, assess and prioritize the risks that you may face. It is followed by applying various resources so that you can control and minimize the risk factors, while businessmen monitoring them. It also includes doing certain things so that you not only reduce the risk but also maximize your opportunities through effective application of resources.

For an everyday trader, it is essential not to risk too much money on any given trade. Unfortunately, most people don't see the risks, but only the potential rewards.

Give it a thought. If a trader was to lose a little bit of money on every transaction, won't he decide to stay for longer? Huge losses are one of the major reasons why so many traders give up. But then why do traders give up? If all big losses start small, isn't it easier to prevent this small loss from becoming uncontrollable? The answer is "YES."

Below we shall see the way to assess risks and hence manage them better.

The importance and benefits of

risk management

One of the major disadvantages of investing money in the stock exchange is the risk that comes along with it. No one is guaranteed success in the stock exchange and you will need to jump into it knowing the risks. Once you assess the risks, you can take precautionary steps to manage these risks. Risk management is extremely important while engaging in day trading and it can make or break your trade. If you are someone who generally takes risks then the stock market is a place where you can invest. Always keep in mind that in day trading the risk doubles and be prepared to manage this risk.

Here are some benefits that day traders will gain once they understand the risks:

- They will be prepared to face financial losses and will have strategies in place to overcome these losses.
- They will learn not to keep their stocks overnight as prices change radically overnight.
- They will realize it's a stressful and time-consuming job and have effective coping strategies in place.
- They will realize that they can't take extreme risks with borrowed money.
- They don't believe in quick profits and promises. They realize that it will take

time and effort.
- They pay close attention to trends and know when something works for them and when it doesn't.

Basic Risk Management in day trading:

- You should be aware of both the potential risks and rewards before you enter a trade. Make sure that the potential rewards outweigh the potential risks.
- You must cut your losses before they become too much. You can either do this manually or through a broker.
- Take position sizes that are appropriate for you. This varies from one trader to the next.
- Don't give in to your pride. This could be a reason for losing money. Everyone who works with the stock market faces losses in the stock market. Don't blame yourself for the loss.

Chapter Summary:

1. In this chapter, you were introduced to risk management and the rationale behind it.
2. You also read about the importance of risk management and the benefits associated with it.

3. You saw the steps that a beginner day trader can take to manage their risks while day trading.

Your Quick Start Action Step:

In this chapter, I urged you to try and implement one of the simple risk management steps mentioned above. Gradually you can try to implement all these steps while you engage in day trading.

Chapter 8:
Day Trading
Tools

Chapter 8: Day Trading Tools
Day Trading prediction techniques

There are certain Day trading techniques or tools (as we like to call them) that you can utilize to forecast the pattern that the stocks will follow.

Candlesticks

These are the most widely used techniques of prediction. Hence, we shall have a detailed look into candlesticks in the next chapter.

Fibonacci numbers

The mathematical technique that is utilized to predict stocks is the Fibonacci technique. Once you know how a Fibonacci series works, you will find it easy to comprehend. Your securities and stocks will follow a Fibonacci pattern and this will help you identify where it will stop next. Using this knowledge you can choose either to stay or withdraw.

Rebate trading

Rebate trading is a popular technique. In this technique, you will be trading via an electronic communication network. These ECNs have been constructed to help people invest their money with ease. Once everybody's money is pooled together, the ECN will invest it in the stock market. It is found to be safe and helpful.

Range trading

Range trading is another good prediction technique. It is necessary to have boundaries and work within a range. To do this you will have to set limits to your investments. You can choose your limits.

Price action

In price action technique we make predictions by looking at the current prices. The trader makes some assumptions. If he thinks that those prices are falling and will continue to fall, he won't invest in them. If he feels those prices are rising and will continue to rise, he will not invest in it. This is an extremely safe approach and works only if one pays close attention to the trends.

Contrarian trading

Contrarian trading means doing the opposite of what the crowd is doing. Here, you buy stocks when people are selling them and sell stocks when people are buying them. This risk usually pays off but you need to know when to carry it out.

News forecasts

You should keep track of the news articles to be aware of the changes that are occurring in the company. If the share value is going up the company announces profits and dividends. On the other hand, if the share value will go down the company announces that it has undergone a loss and the steps it will take to minimize the effect of the loss or how they will rebuild. You need to work with this knowledge.

Software

There are different kinds of software that will help you with your stock investments. You have to see which works best for you. They help you read and predict the trends. This software can be installed by you on your own or with the help of a friend or broker.

The other essentials tools are a good computer or laptop, good telephone connection and a fast Internet connection.

Importance of using these day trading tools:

These are the different prediction techniques that you must take into account to be successful in day trading. You can choose any of these day trading tools to help you in your venture. In today's world, you cannot expect to succeed without the help of these tools. You require technology to assist you in your trades.

Some of the benefits of these tools are:

- Gives you an edge over other investors in the market.

- Will help you save time and energy
- Will help in the formation an advantageous strategy and increase your chances of being successful.

How Fibonacci numbers can help you trade better:

1. Some academics agree that Fibonacci numbers are powerful in financial markets.
2. These numbers offer a framework for evaluating price action
3. These numbers are watched by traders and provide key horizontal price levels.
4. These price levels tend to bring higher levels or more volume and thus, can lead to a promising trade setup.

Chapter Summary:

1. You had a look at the different types of day trading tools and the benefits associated with them.
2. You read about the importance of implementing these day trading tools in your trade
3. You also saw how Fibonacci numbers candlesticks help you become a better trader.

Your Quick Start Action Step:

In this chapter, I suggest that you check out and try using Fibonacci numbers. If you want, you can also check out the other tools mentioned in section 8.1.

Chapter 9:
Candlesticks

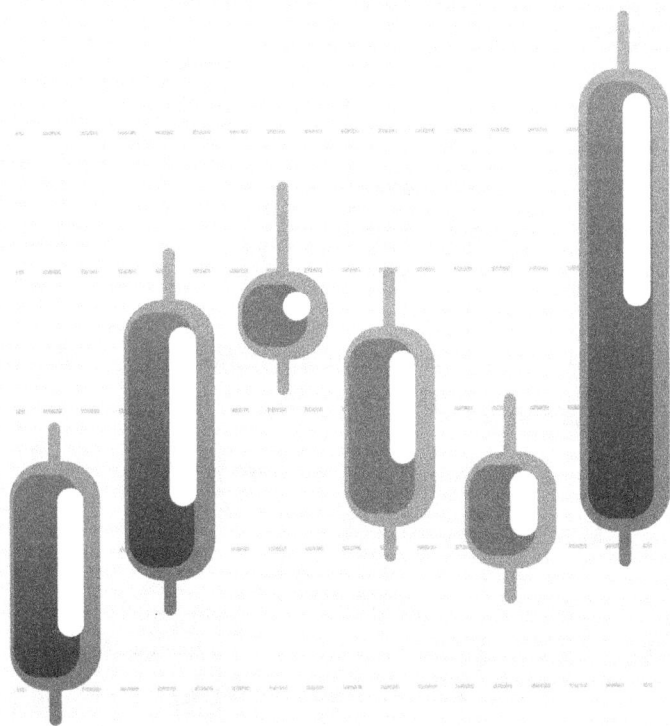

Chapter 9: Candlesticks

Candlesticks and Day Trading:

A candlestick chart can be described as a financial chart that is usually used to study the movement of the prices of derivatives, currencies or security. Each candlestick represents a single day.

It is thought that a Japanese rice trader called Munehisa Homma developed Candlestick charts in the 18th Century. Steve Nison introduced these charts to the Western world through his book, Japanese Candlestick Charting Techniques. Candle Stick are now often used in stock analysis in addition to other analytical tools like Fibonacci numbers

Importance of Candlestick patterns:

The candlestick strategy is widely known and used by experienced traders. Centuries ago rice traders from Japan found that an investor's emotion about an asset involved in trade seems to have a profound effect on the movement of that asset's. With the help of candlesticks, traders measure the emotions associated with a stock, and this helps them make better predictions as to which direction that stock could be headed in.

- This technique is simple, and it is easy to follow and comprehend.
- The trader bases his decision on prediction.
- The pattern is best suited for traders who would prefer to use a technical approach.
- These traders trade based on predictions and patterns.

How to use candlestick techniques in day trading:

1. In this trading strategy patterns for particular stocks are created depending on its "HOD" or highest of the day prices and "LOD" or lowest of day prices.
2. A graph is plotted with the help of these statistics.
3. A technique called doji reversal pattern is used. This helps in making proper candlesticks.
4. After the establishment of the candlesticks, the pattern that the stock is believed to follow will be identified by the trader.
5. Once this has been done, the trader will predict whether the price will either rise or fall.
6. Then the trader will either decide to sell the stock or hold onto it.

You can do more extensive research on this topic if required.

Chapter Summary:

1. In this chapter, we got acquainted with what candlesticks are. We read about the history of candlesticks.
2. The importance and benefits of candlestick patterns were briefly discussed.
3. The steps that a trader can use to implement the candlesticks technique in his day to day trading were also discussed.

Your Quick Start Action Step:

In this chapter, I urge you to take some time out of your schedule try implementing the steps mentioned in section 9.3

Chapter 10: Day Trading with Penny Stocks

Chapter 10: Day Trading with Penny Stocks

Penny Stocks and day trading:

Today in day trading the most preferred kinds of stocks are penny stocks. Stocks that are valued at $5 or less are called "penny stocks." Even though they are called as cent or penny stocks, they are rarely valued so cheaply.

Penny stocks became very famous when a trader named Jordan Belfort transformed his hundreds of dollars into millions by trading in penny stocks. Although he did become a millionaire overnight, he later confessed that he controlled the stock market illegally.

A person can make money in the penny stock market using lawful means. However, it takes a lot of commitment and patience to see positive results as these stocks are not found in the stock market and are exchanged over the counter. Big stock markets don't encourage them owing to the fact that they are extremely volatile and priced very low. These stocks are not your usual everyday stocks and hence, are distributed through the pink sheet system.

You can purchase these stocks by buying the sheets and trading with them. Agents, who are authorized to, can get these stocks for you as they have access to them. However, you will have to inform them in advance so that they can make the necessary arrangements.

Importance of penny stocks:

The risks associated with penny stocks sometimes overweigh the benefits. There is just so much misinformation considering penny stocks. It is crucial that a person who wishes to become a successful trader should know about the true potential risks and profits associated with this trading strategy. It is essential that you gather the right information and use this trading strategy to help you become a better day trader. By knowing the ins and outs of penny stocks you can avoid the loss of time and money that comes with the lack of knowledge.

- You will know all the risks and benefits associated with penny stocks.
- You will learn how to predict penny stocks.
- You will save time and money. You can use this time and money for other pursuits.
- The low cost enables you to buy a larger number of stocks.
- Penny stocks tend to have a greater return potential than well-established companies.

General Steps of day trading with

penny stocks:

Predicting penny stocks

Like with most other stocks, the best way to make money is to predict the pattern of the stocks. Once you have successfully predicted in which direction the stocks are headed- whether they will rise or fall, you have the chance to protect your investment, while also making the most out of it.

We have already looked at different prediction methods that you can use to predict the movement of your stocks. These techniques that we have seen can be applied to your penny stocks as well. Apart from those techniques, here are some more techniques that you can try.

Change in volume

If you happen to notice any unusual change in the volume of the stock, you must look into the cause. This is also a sign for you to invest in a particular stock, as the value of the stock is sure to rise. There needs to be a dramatic rise in the volume for any consequential change to occur in it. Therefore, you must keep track of all the stocks that you own and must also bookmark stocks that you wish to own.

Flow of money

The next thing to pay attention to is amount of

money that is put into the company. If a lot of money has been funded by the company then it becomes a good place to invest. You should pay close attention to the news to how much money has been invested and where it has come from. Usually, if you know how much money has been invested in the company, you can decide how much you want to invest. But, don't do this without performing different technical and fundamental analyses.

Market capture

The stock's overall presence in the market is referred to as market share or market capture. Have a look at the number of shares of the company that is being traded in the market. You must also make inquiries by calling the customer support team. If the market share of the company is big, then it is more likely to do well. However, you shouldn't base your decision on this one criterion alone. You have to do more research.

Name game

If the company you are thinking of buying into is advertised in the media, for one reason or the other, then it is most likely going to do well. Most times, the news will be negative, but because of this news, the company receives publicity. So, irrespective of what the news is about, if a company's name is being advertised over media, then its stocks will most likely do well.

Product launch

If the penny stock company that you invested in launches something new, the stock prices could rise. If the product is being launched on a huge scale then the chances that the stock will do well are high. You need to pay attention to such news. Keep in mind that penny stock companies may not be as large as regular companies, but they will be large enough to reach the news.

Anticipation

The power of anticipation is a tool that you can capitalize on. This means that you shouldn't wait to buy the shares just before a company announces its results. Once the results are announced, a sort of buying frenzy takes place. Most people won't even bother to check if the results are positive or negative, but they will buy in bulk. You have to correctly time your sales during such periods. When the demand for the stock increases, you should sell them in the market.

In the end, you can decide whether or not to invest in penny stocks. However, I encourage you to do further research and gather more information about penny stocks before making your decision.

Chapter Summary:

1. In this chapter, you read about the relationship between penny stocks and day trading and the origins of penny stocks.
2. The importance of learning about Penny Stocks for a person who wants to succeed in this field was also explained in detail.
3. You also saw the general steps of day trading with penny stocks.

Your Quick Start Action Step:

We've almost reached the end of our book. Hope this book has been helpful so far. In this chapter, I urge you to try the steps mentioned in section 10.3.

Bonus Chapter: Day Trading for Investors

Bonus Chapter: Day Trading for Investors

Day Trading for Investors:

Most people seem to use the terms "trading" and "investing" conversely when, in truth, both the terms are very different. While investors and traders both work the same marketplace, their tasks and strategies are very different. However, both these parties are required for the smooth functioning of the market

Traders trading styles often depend upon aspects like experience of the trader, size of the account, amount of time that is devoted to trading, tolerance of risk and personality. Both traders and investors try to make profits by participating in the market. Generally, an investor looks for bigger profits over an extended period of time. This is done via buying and holding stocks for long periods. Whereas on the other end, traders make use of the rise and fall of the financial market to enter or exit a position. Traders usually work over a smaller time period and take more frequent and smaller profits.

Day trading is found at the extreme end of the investing spectrum as it is very different from the usual "buy-and-hold wisdom". Investors may engage in day trading and traders might engage in investing. But, the results of investment are more certain and come with a lesser risk. Hence, most investors do not seek to become traders. But, they can do so with the knowledge they possess about the stock market and the information given above.

Importance of learning the concept of day trading:

Day trading is only a good idea for an investor if he has a large amount of money that he can invest. Irrespective of how long or short your time frame is, whether you are a novice or an experienced day trader, you are not going to succeed unless you have a written plan with risk management, manage your money.

The reason why day trading is considered as such a risky venture is because of that fact that people who think they can day trade don't have the necessary knowledge to help them. They choose not to learn much about day trading. This puts them at a disadvantage. Investors usually work the market long term. Only with the necessary knowledge can they learn to work the market short term as in the case of day trading.

Investors that usually make money in the market do it by carefully evaluating the stocks they are about to purchase. But, sometimes even experienced day traders and investors lose from time to time. It happens!

Features of successful day traders:

- They gain extra knowledge about trading.
- They learn the variations between investing and trading.
- They can venture and try out business opportunities in both fields.
- They learn how to play the market both short and long term.

Steps on day trading for investors:

The way in which an investor day trades is very similar to the way in which a beginner day trader trades. But, in the former case, these investors already possess knowledge concerning the stock market and do not enter this game without prior experience. Some of the strategies that they learned in investing can be applied to trading.

1. Try to read up more and gain more information about day trading
2. Get a good computer. Install a good day trading software onto this computer.
3. Read up on the basics of trading and investing. Learn to differentiate between both concepts.

4. Learn additional strategies and concepts that can help you day trade better. (ECN's, candlesticks, order routing, brokerage, technical analysis, etc.).
5. Once this is done, enlist the help of a broker from a good brokerage firm to set up an account that you can use for trading stocks and securities. Currencies can also, for trading.
6. The next step is to begin paper-trading stocks (or currencies).
7. Voila! You're done. Go on and have fun day trading.

Chapter Summary:

1. In this chapter, you read about concept of investors in day trading.
2. You saw the reasons why investors need to learn about day trading even though it involves "Trading" instead of "Investing".
3. The general steps that an investor could follow to become a day trader have also been listed in this chapter.

Your Quick Start Action Step:

In this chapter, I urge to have a look at this website. I hope the information presented in this website helps you.

https://www.tradeking.com/investing/basics-of-day-trading

Conclusion

Thank you again once again for purchasing this book!

I hope this book was able to help you find what you've been looking for. I also hope that this book helped you gain valuable information on options trading.

It is quite vital to remember the fact that options trading is only rewarding if you do it in good order. The risks are plenty, but then again when is anything ever risk-free? Therefore, it is up to you to take control of the situation with the invaluable information I have provided you with. Day trading opens many doors for you (a normal person) to make some or maybe even truckloads of big bucks. You don't have to be an Einstein to decipher what day trading is. It's quite simple, really.

In his book, "The Great Pearl of Wisdom", Bangambiki Habyarimana has stated, "Opportunity and risk come in pairs." Hence, only if one is willing to take lots of risks will he be able to get a higher yield. However, not many would be prepared to undertake such risk. So, for one that is not ready to take that big leap, start slowly and see if Day Trading is really your forte. Once you are sure of your decision you can go all the way.

I trust that that this book was a means for you to know anything and everything that will make day trading a reality for you. I also believe that it will push you to not only step into the massive world of trading but will also ensure that when you leave it, you do not leave without the stacks of green bills that you've always wished to have.

Happy Investing!

About the Author

Warren Richmond is a professional trader and investment professional of 10 years.

When he was in college, he got interested in trading and investing early but got frustrated understanding the highly complex topic.

Warren wanted a teaching method that he could easily learn from and develop his trading and investing skills. He soon discovered a teaching series that made him learn faster and better.

Applying the same approach, Warren successfully learned the necessary skills in order to become a professional trader and is now teaching the subject matter through writing books.

With the books that he writes on trading, he hopes to provide great value and help readers interested to learn trading.

www.ingramcontent.com/pod-product-compliance
Lightning Source LLC
Chambersburg PA
CBHW071435210326
41597CB00020B/3798

www.ingramcontent.com/pod-product-compliance
Lightning Source LLC
Chambersburg PA
CBHW071435210326
41597CB00020B/3798